STOCK

INVESTING

*"A Beginners Guide On How To
Invest On Stock Market"*

By

LYNN WALKER

The information herein is offered for informational purposes solely and is universal as so. The presentation of the information is without a contract or any type of guarantee assurance.

The trademarks that are used are without any consent, and the publication of the trademark is without permission or backing by the trademark owner. All trademarks and brands within this book are for clarifying purposes only and are owned by the owners themselves, not affiliated with this document

Table of Contents

INTRODUCTION

Many people, just like you, turn to the markets to help buy a home, send children to college, or build a retirement nest egg. But unlike the banking world, where deposits are guaranteed by federal deposit insurance, the value of stocks, bonds, and other securities fluctuates with market conditions. No one can guarantee that you'll make money from your investments, and they may lose value.

Returns over the past year have struggled to gain momentum, with active fund managers seeking cautious investment stances amid the persistent waves of volatility. One of the best investment returns of the year would surely have gone to those on the winning side of the 5000 to 1 odds given to Leicester winning the Premier League. Luckily the Investment process does not resolve to luck, and hereunder I will run you through some considerations Investment managers undertake prior to setting Investment strategies.

Investment management can take an active or passive approach to generate investment returns. The latter, however, would generally consist of replicating a reference benchmark with e ual weightings and asset holdings. Examples of passive investment strategies include Index funds and Exchange Traded Funds (ETFs).

Most investors tend to enjoy maximum yielding returns, and many funds take on active investment management strategies within a fund's terms of operation to cater to such demands. Active investment management seeks to generate value-added returns in excess to returns on a reference benchmark, better known as alpha in technical terms.

Ratios that fund managers usually use in assessing the active value-added risk in a portfolio include the Information ratio and the Sharpe ratio. The former measures the mean active risk-return per unit of active risk. To keep it simple, it measures the ability of a manager to beat the benchmark relative to volatility.

For example, assuming a benchmark portfolio gives a weighting of 10 % to an asset class, a fund manager believing the asset class has upside potential going forward, can replicate the positions in a benchmark but assign a higher weighting to such an asset class. This investment strategy would be called taking an overweight exposure to the asset class. The same concept applies to the opposite, whereby investment managers can take on underweight positions.

The Sharpe ratio, considered more popular, measures the excess return over the risk-free rate (usually the rate on a US Treasury bill) per unit of total portfolio risk. By total portfolio risk, I refer to the degree of the tendency of returns being dispersed from the mean returns of a portfolio.

Besides the weightings attributed to respective asset classes and positions within a portfolio, investment managers assess the factor sensitivities on the underlying constituents through the use of multi-factor models. Factor sensitivities constitute mainly systematic (market) risk factors, that is, the risk factors in a portfolio that cannot be eliminated through added diversification of investment holdings.

A key in any portfolio is to have a well-diversified investment strategy. The larger the number of holdings in a portfolio, the greater the chance of eliminating asset-specific risk factors and remaining with what is called systematic risk, given correlation is low amongst the selected positions.

Multi-22factor models assess all factors affecting the potential returns on an underlying holding. For example, inflation and GDP growth are non-diversifiable market factors that would largely affect cyclical stocks and high yield holdings in a portfolio. These holdings, as a result, would be given a higher sensitivity factor by management in analyzing the expected returns on the underlying constituents.

The above is an apercu of part of the analysis put forward by investment management teams in generating returns. The past year has proved challenging, and given ongoing volatility, the search for yield will remain subdued, not given a turn in market growth and consumer confidence.

Having said that, a global recovery will hopefully improve given the latest easing of monetary policy.

Investors, therefore, can remain confident in generating future returns other than predicting the next unlikely winner of the English premier league.

WHAT IS INVESTMENT

An investment is a purchase that is completed with money that has the potential to produce income or a profit. Things that naturally lose value over time and with use are not investments.

An investor is a person or entity who outlays capital in order to produce an income or to make profits. Investing is the act of putting forth capital with the expectation of income or profit. Personal investing is buying financial securities or property for the purpose of making a profit.

Most investments earn investor money through appreciation, interest payments, or dividends. Appreciation means that the value of an asset has increased. If you purchased a collectible item for $100 and five years later it was worth $500, then the collectible appreciated in value. Securities can do the same -- a stock issued by a company can increase in value over a number of years.

You've likely paid interest payments on a loan you've taken out, whether that was a student loan or mortgage. These interest payments you paid the lender were how the lender earned money on that loan (or investment). One type of security that issues interest payments to its investors is a bond. When you buy a bond, you are lending money to the government or a corporation, who promises to pay you back and make interest payments on the amount you lent.

Dividends are also issued as a payment to investors, but they are made by companies whose stock or e□uity that you own. Public companies issue stock to raise money for business activities, letting investors purchase these stocks. If you own stock in a company, that company may also issue dividend payments to you as a way to share its profits with its investors. This is on top of any appreciation in the value of the stock.

TYPES OF INVESTMENTS

As an investor, you have a lot of options for where to put your money. It's important to weigh them carefully.

Investments are generally bucketed into three major categories: stocks, bonds, and cash e☐uivalents. There are many ways to invest in each bucket.

Here are six types of investments you might consider for long-term growth, and what you should know about each. Note: We won't get into cash e☐uivalents — things like money markets, certificates of deposit or savings accounts — as they're less about growing your money and more about keeping it safe.

Stocks

A stock is an investment in a specific company. When you purchase a stock, you're buying a share — a small piece — of that company's earnings and assets. Companies sell shares of stock in their businesses to raise cash; investors can then buy and sell those shares among themselves. Stocks sometimes earn high returns but also come with more risk than other investments. Companies can lose value or go out of business.

How investors make money: Stock investors make money when the value of the stock they own goes up, and they're able to sell that stock for a profit. Some stocks also pay dividends, which are regular distributions of a company's earnings to investors.

Bonds

A bond is a loan you make to a company or government. When you purchase a bond, you're allowing the bond issuer to borrow your money and pay you back with interest. Bonds are generally considered safer than stocks, but they also offer lower returns. The primary risk, as with any loan, is that the issuer could default. U.S. government bonds are backed by the "full faith and credit" of the United States, which effectively eliminates that risk. State and city government bonds are generally considered the next-safest option, followed by corporate bonds—the safer the bond, the lower the interest rate.

How investors make money: Bonds are a fixed-income investment, because investors expect regular income payments. Interest is generally paid to investors in regular instalments — typically once or twice a year — and the total principal is paid off at the bond's maturity date.

Mutual funds

If the idea of picking and choosing individual bonds and stocks isn't your bag, you're not alone. In fact, there's an investment designed just for people like you: the mutual fund.

Mutual funds allow investors to purchase a large number of investments in a single transaction. These funds pool money from many investors, then employ a professional manager to invest that money in stocks, bonds, or other assets.

Mutual funds follow a set strategy — a fund might invest in a specific type of stocks or bonds, like international stocks or government bonds. Some funds invest in both stocks and bonds. How risky the mutual fund is will depend on the investments within the fund.

How investors make money: When a mutual fund earns money — for example, through stock dividends or bond interest — it distributes a proportion of that to investors. When investments in the fund go up in value, the value of the fund increases as well, which means you could sell it for a profit. Note that you'll pay an annual fee, called an expense ratio, to invest in a mutual fund.

Index funds

An index fund is a type of mutual fund that passively tracks an index, rather than paying a manager to pick and choose investments. For example, an S&P 500 index fund will aim to mirror the performance of the S&P 500 by holding stock of the companies within that index.

The benefit of index funds is that they tend to cost less because they don't have that active manager on the payroll. The risk associated with an index fund will depend on the investments within the fund.

How investors make money: Index funds may earn dividends or interest, which is distributed to investors. These funds may also go up in value when the benchmark indexes they track go up in value; investors can then sell their share in the fund for a profit. Index funds also charge expense ratios, but as noted above, these costs tend to be lower than mutual fund fees.

Exchange-traded funds

ETFs are a type of index fund: They track a benchmark index and aim to mirror that index's performance. Like index funds, they tend to be cheaper than mutual funds because they are not actively managed.

The major difference between index funds and ETFs is how ETFs are purchased: They trade on an exchange like a stock, which means you can buy and sell ETFs throughout the day and an ETF's price will fluctuate throughout the day. Mutual funds and index funds, on the other hand, are priced once at the end of each trading day — that price will be the same no matter what time you buy or sell. Bottom line: This difference doesn't matter to many investors, but if you want more control over the price of the fund, you might prefer an ETF.

How investors make money: As with a mutual fund and an index fund, your hope as an investor is that the fund will increase in value, and you'll be able to sell it for a profit. ETFs may also pay out dividends and interest to investors.

Options

An option is a contract to buy or sell a stock at a set price by a set date. Options offer flexibility, as the contract doesn't actually obligate you to buy or sell the stock. As the name implies, doing so is an option. Most options contracts are for 100 shares of stock. When you buy an option, you're buying the contract, not the stock itself. You can then either buy or sell the stock at the agreed-upon price within the agreed-upon time, sell the options contract to another investor, or let the contract expire.

How investors make money: Options can be quite complex, but at a basic level, you are locking in the price of a stock you expect to increase in value. If your crystal ball is right, you benefit by purchasing the stock for less than the going rate. If it is wrong, you can forgo the purchase, and you're only out the cost of the contract itself.

Risks With Investing

Even though investing can earn money for you, it is not without risks. The biggest risk of investing is that you may lose the money you invested. Unlike savings or checking accounts, whose value is guaranteed by the Federal Deposit Insurance Corporation (FDIC), investments have no such guarantee.

Certain investments are less risky than others, but all investments carry some amount of risk. The amount of risk also affects the rate of return of an investment, meaning for someone to take on a lot of risks, there must also be the possibility of great reward. Think about it: you wouldn't take a big risk without the possibility of a big payoff. Conversely, investments with less risk typically have lower returns.

One way that investors reduce their overall risk is by investing in a variety of different securities, such as stocks and bonds, or even in different types of the same security, such as government bonds and corporate bonds. This is known as diversification, and it's an important concept for any investor to understand.

Another big risk in investing in your own emotions. Many investments are volatile in the short term, meaning that their value may fluctuate a lot over one to five years. During economic recessions, the value of many investments may fall dramatically. As an investor, it is difficult to watch your investments lose money. This can lead to investment decisions based on fear or panic, such as selling stocks, when the prices fall too low for your comfort.

When you invest, you should be holding most of your investments for ten, twenty, or more years. It's over these longer time periods that the value of investments has historically increased. The Standard and Poor's 500 (S&P 500), a stock market index, averaged a 7% inflation-adjusted return from 1950 to 2020. Keep this in mind when you make investing decisions. You'll perform better as an investor if your investment decisions are based on logic and reason rather than emotions.

You may have heard investing compared to gambling, and if you invest in a lackadaisical way, it may be the same. However, smart investors will approach investing strategically to choose investments that have a good expectation of return. Gambling, on the other hand, is usually based purely on chance.

In order to minimize risk, you can utilize asset allocation in your portfolio. This refers to the apportionment of capital assets in a way that balances the risks and rewards.

Fees

Fees are monies that are charged to your account that should appear on your contract and statement. Commissions are charged by brokers in exchange for them placing trades on behalf of the account holders. Management expenses are for managing your securities. Transaction costs are for each time that you buy or sell a security. Annual costs are fees on a yearly basis for keeping your account open.

Various charges can add up and offset returns. It is important to read your statements and be aware of all the brokerage fees. Another fee to watch is the expense ratio. This is an annual fee expressed as a percentage of your investment. It is inherent in mutual funds, exchange-traded funds, and index funds. It can substantially lower your portfolio returns.

Return on investment (ROI)

Your return on investment represents the financial gain or profitability percentage from an investment over a period of time. It is used in finance to compare the efficiency of different investments and is also used in conjunction with other methods of

27

measuring your return. You can also calculate your ROI by using an ROI calculator.

Research your investment

Research helps you to stay informed on investments and the market. To stay current with the most recent information, you should read the best investment books, the best investment bloggers, and the best investment and financial websites.

Be realistic about the performance expectations that you have about the best investments for you. Your expectations and objectives should not be about how to get rich ☐uickly but should instead be focused on how to get rich slowly. You should take a long-term view, and you should invest as early as you can and as much as you can. Many get-rich-quick investments are fraudulent, so you should watch out for them.

STOCK MARKET CAPITALIZATION

Market capitalization, or market cap, is the total value of a company's stock within the stock market. Calculating a publicly-traded company's market cap is easy: Just take the number of shares of stock the company has issued and multiply it by the current market price of the stock. So if a company has issued a total of 2 million outstanding shares and each share is valued at $20, then the company's total market capitalization is $40 million.

But why is market cap important, and how should you use it? Market cap is one of the best measures of a company's size, and size can tell you a lot about what to expect if you buy its stock.

In general, large companies tend to have more stable and mature businesses, having proven themselves over time and weathered difficult business conditions to emerge stronger. However, the growth prospects for large companies tend to be more limited because they've already taken advantage of their primary opportunities to grow to their current size.

By contrast, smaller companies have a lot more room to grow. However, smaller companies tend to be younger, with riskier business models that haven't yet proved themselves over time. Their odds of failure are significantly higher than those of larger companies.

Here's a □uick breakdown of the way market capitalization ranges are often segmented and discussed within the stock market:

What are large-cap stocks?

Large-cap stocks have market capitalizations of $10 billion or more. Most of the best-known companies in the world are large caps, and some investors break out stocks with market caps of more than $200 billion into a separate category as mega-cap stocks.

Most large-cap companies have mature business models and generate substantial amounts of revenue. They often earn significant profits and have a considerable market share within their industries, making them leaders in their fields. They're more likely than smaller companies to pay sizable dividends to their shareholders because their businesses tend to produce greater amounts of available cash.

On the other hand, large-cap companies have often already gone through their period of maximum growth. As a result, even successful large-cap companies that pay healthy dividends and whose shares go up in value consistently won't always be able to match the massive returns that smaller companies can achieve.

What are mid-cap stocks?

Mid-cap stocks have market caps in the range of $2 billion to $10 billion, occupying the middle ground between large and small companies. Mid-cap companies are large enough to have made considerable progress in building up successful business models, and that gives their investors some stability and protection against future challenges those companies will face. However, they're small enough that they give investors a longer runway for future growth than a large-cap stock. That said, mid-caps also face the difficult task of catching up to and surpassing larger rivals in their industries, and they don't have as many financial resources at their disposal.

It's important when investing in mid-cap stocks to know their history. Some mid-cap companies are still in their high-growth phase, while others have reached their full potential in relatively small niche industries of limited size. Still, others are older companies that used to be large-caps but have seen their businesses lose steam. Any of these can be good investments under the right circumstances, but they can have very different characteristics in terms of growth potential, dividend income, and valuation.

What are small-cap stocks?

Small-cap stocks have market capitalizations of between $300 million and $2 billion. Some people also include within this category even smaller companies with market capitalizations of $50 million to

$300 million, while others put those tiny stocks into a separate group as micro-cap stocks. Small-cap companies tend to be younger than large caps or mid-caps, and they often have a much shorter track record as operating businesses. Small caps often have considerable growth potential, but investors in small caps face a lot more uncertainty about their future. In many cases, small caps have to upend much larger competitors in order to stake their claims within a given industry, and for every small company that succeeds, many fail.

Over time, small-cap stocks have historically produced higher average returns than large-cap stocks, but their performance has been more volatile along the way. That reuires small-cap investors to have a greater risk tolerance than those who concentrate on larger stocks. Those with long time horizons can typically weather the

35

ups and downs of small-cap stocks and therefore have a better chance of enjoying the reward of greater returns.

How To Use Market Cap

Most investors find that having a diversified portfolio that includes large-cap, mid-cap, and small-cap stocks let them tailor their desired return and risk levels to their specific wishes. If you want your portfolio to be more stable, then you'll want a larger allocation to large-cap stocks. Those who want greater amounts of current income will also typically gravitate to large caps. By contrast, if you don't need much income and your primary goal is to have your portfolio grow as much as it can over many years, then you'll likely want to make larger investment allocations to small-cap and mid-cap stocks.

THE STRENGTHS AND WEAKNESSES OF STOCK MARKET CAPITALIZATION

Stock prices can sometimes be misleading when comparing one company to another. Stock market capitalization, on the other hand, ignores capital structure specifics that can cause the share price of one firm to be higher than another. This allows investors to understand the two companies' relative sizes. For example, compare Coca-Cola at $53.75 per share with streaming service Netflix at $276.82 per share. Despite having an exponentially larger share price, the latter has a stock market capitalization of roughly $121 billion, more than $100 billion smaller than Coke's. This illustrates some of the complications that come with how to think about share price. Sometimes, a $300 stock might be cheaper than a $10 stock.

On the flip side, stock market capitalization is limited in what it can tell you. The biggest downfall of this particular metric is that it does not factor into consideration a company's debt. Consider Coca-Cola once more. At the end of 2018, the company had around $29.2 billion in current liabilities (debt, taxes, etc.). If you were to buy the entire business, you would be responsible for servicing and repaying all those liabilities. That means, while Coke's stock market capitalization is $230 billion, it's enterprise value is $259.2 billion. All else being e□ual, the latter figure is what you would need to not only buy all of the common stock—but pay off all the company's debt, too. Enterprise value is a more accurate indicator of determining the takeover value of a company.

Another major weakness of using stock market capitalization as a proxy for a company's performance is that it does not factor in distributions such as spin-offs, split-offs, or dividends, which are extremely important in calculating a concept known as the "total return." It seems strange to many new investors, but the total return can result in an investor making money, even if the company itself goes bankrupt. For one, you may have collected dividends over the years. The company could also get bought out, and your shares could be bought outright or transferred to shares in the new parent company.

ADVANTAGES OF USING A MARKET CAPITALIZATION

The market capitalization method is the easiest and most popular form of determining the market worth of a business. It measures the size of a business by multiplying the price per share by the number of shares in existence. There is a slight variant of the market capitalization method that is becoming more popular, and that is the "free float" version of the market capitalization method. This model multiplies the price per share by the number of shares readily available for trading. This method is the one with the most advantages.

Simplicity

market capitalization method has one great advantage: it is simple and direct. Anyone can do it. It is also the most honest. Even if the share prices are distorted because of debt or media-created demand, it reflects the value of the stock as the market sees it. This is all most investors care about.

Size

market capitalization method deals with a firm's size, as seen by the market. If you are an investor who only wants relatively safe and stable investments, then the market capitalization method is the only model you will use. This is because what is defined as stable is generally limited to the larger-cap stocks such as Wal-Mart. The ☐uickest way to identify the larger, more stable firms is by using the market capitalization method because it deals only in sheer bulk.

Availability

Some investors argue that the free float version of the market capitalization method is important because it improves the basic advantages of the market capitalization method in general. If the great advantage of the market capitalization method is its honest reporting of a firm's worth based on the total amount of issued stock, the free float method is even better because it only deals with what is important to investors: the price of stocks available now.

Demand

The free float mechanism of the market capitalization method reflects market trends better than the market capitalization method by itself. Part of the reason for this is that it reduces the influence of any stocks that are not tradable, and hence not relevant to the market. If the market capitalization method shows a firm the way the market sees it, then market capitalization method-FF is a more accurate indicator of the market trends of the firm. If the shares are inactive, then they tell us nothing about any additional value of the stock deriving from demand or high trading volume. Demand is a part of firm value and should be reflected. Demand is about investor confidence. The free float method more accurately reflects the importance of demand by dealing only with those shares that can, in fact, be demanded.

BLUE CHIPS STOCKS

Investing in blue-chip stocks may have a reputation for being boring, stodgy, and perhaps even a little outdated. However, it isn't an accident that they are overwhelmingly preferred by wealthy investors and rock-solid financial institutions. Anyone with common sense would want a stake in businesses they not only understand but that have a demonstrated record of extreme profitability over generations, and blue chips certainly fit the description. Measured across long periods, blue-chip stocks have minted money for owners prudent enough to hang on to them with tenacity through thick and thin, good times and bad times, war and peace, inflation, and deflation.

And it isn't as if they are unknown. They are ubi␣uitous, taken for granted. Blue-chip stocks often represent companies residing at the core of American and global business; firms boasting pasts every bit as colourful as any novel and interwoven with politics and history. Their products and services permeate nearly every aspect of our lives.

How is it possible, then, those blue-chip stocks have long reigned supreme in the investment portfolios of retirees, non-profit foundations, as well as members of the top 1% and the capitalist class, while being almost entirely ignored by smaller, poorer investors? This conundrum gives us a glimpse into the problem of investment management as it is and even requires some discussion of behavioural economics. Blue-chip stocks don't belong exclusively to the realm of widows and insurance companies, and here's why.

What Is a Blue Chip Stock?

A blue-chip is a stock of a well-established corporation with a reputation for reliability, quality, and financial stability. Blue-chip stocks are usually the market leaders in their sectors and have a market capitalization running into billions of dollars. They are the most popular stocks to buy, due to their long track records of steady earnings or paying dividends. Blue-chip stocks are significant components of some of the world's most reputable indexes such as the Dow Jones Industrial Average, Nasda☐ 100 and S&P 500 in the United States, TSX-60 in Canada and the FTSE in the United Kingdom.

Many stock market investors prefer blue-chip stocks due to their stable earnings. Blue-chip stocks usually pay increasing and consistent dividends over time to at least partially make up for any temporary declines in the stock's price. During economic slowdowns, investors turn to blue-chip stocks to protect their investments. For example, during the financial crisis in the last decade, some blue-chip companies survived the crisis, and investors who held shares in these companies were able to recover their earnings. Investors in blue-chip stocks are generally assured of receiving regular dividend payments and having their portfolios protected against inflation.

Origin Of Blue Chip Stocks

The term "blue chip" was first used to describe high-quality stocks in the early 1920s by a Dow Jones employee, Oliver Gingold. Oliver was standing by the stock ticker at the brokerage firm when he observed some shares trading at $200, $250, or more. He told Lucien Hooper of W.E. Hutton & Co. that he planned to go back to the office and write about "these blue-chip stocks." The term's been used since then to refer to high-priced stocks, just as blue chips in poker typically carry higher chip values. Blue-chip stocks do not necessarily need to be highly-priced but should be of high □uality.

How To Invest In Blue Chip Stocks?

Before buying stocks, you should consult an investment advisor, or another professional advisor, in addition to performing your own research on the best-performing companies. Evaluate the recent annual and □uarterly published reports of stocks to understand their performance and any changes in the management of the company. Analyze the company's performance for the last decade to know the dividend payments trend and the reported earnings. Looking at the historical performance over a long period of time will give a more precise indication of a company's performance during both boom and bust cycles. Compare several high-quality stocks and decide which ones to invest in based on your stock evaluations and your personal investment goals. The SEC recommends stock diversification to minimize risks, and you can choose several premier stocks to start with.

You can purchase stocks individually through a brokerage firm or buy a basket of stocks by investing in mutual funds or ETFs. If you are buying stocks through a brokerage, you can choose an online broker, a full-service broker, or a discount broker depending on the level of personal service you desire. Once an account is opened and you have provided all the necessary documentation, you will need to make a deposit with the broker. You can then place your first buy order for the number of shares you want to buy of a given stock.

Some mutual funds or ETFs use "Blue Chip" in their name and contain a list of the best-performing stocks in various sectors. For example, Bridgeway Blue Chip 35 Index invests more in technology companies and less in consumer discretionary companies. Vanguard's Dividend Appreciation ETF (VIG) tracks the Dividend Achievers Select Index, an index that lists U.S. companies that have increased their dividend payments in the last ten or more consecutive years.

BENEFITS OF BLUE CHIP STOCKS

Blue-chip stocks are generally considered to provide a safe harbour during economic downtowns. Some of the companies listed on the Dow Jones index, such as Coca-Cola, General Electric, and Procter and Gamble company, have survived major economic slowdowns well over the years due to their strong balance sheet and excellent management teams. Such companies are capable of buying out and driving out weak competitors after a crisis, therefore strengthening their financial position even more. As previously noted, blue-chip stocks typically pay consistent and steady dividends to their investors. Research shows that dividend-paying stocks tend to be less affected in bear markets. Investors can sometimes live off the dividend payouts during their retirement and pass on the wealth of their stock holdings to their children when they die.

Some investors love buying blue-chip stocks on the theory that the strength of the financial statements of the issuing companies means that their income is protected. Inexperienced investors often target investments that they think will make them rich quickly. More experienced investors, especially those who have already acquired wealth, tend to focus more on establishing sustained income for the future and on protecting their existing wealth with stable investments, even if those investments only offer a more modest rate of return.

What Are The Names Of Some Blue Chip Stocks?

Despite there not being universal agreement about what constitutes a blue-chip stock. Generally, some names you are going to find on most people's list, as well as the rosters of white-glove asset management firms, include corporations such as:

- ✓ 3M
- ✓ American Express
- ✓ AT&T
- ✓ Berkshire Hathaway
- ✓ Boeing
- ✓ Chevron
- ✓ The Clorox Company
- ✓ The Coca-Cola Company
- ✓ Colgate-Palmolive
- ✓ Diageo
- ✓ Exxon Mobil
- ✓ General Electric
- ✓ The Hershey Company
- ✓ Johnson & Johnson
- ✓ Kraft Heinz
- ✓ McDonald's Corporation
- ✓ Nestle SA
- ✓ PepsiCo
- ✓ Procter & Gamble
- ✓ United Technologies
- ✓ Visa

- ✓ Wal-Mart Stores
- ✓ The Walt Disney Company
- ✓ Wells Fargo & Company

From time to time, you'll find a situation where a former blue-chip stock goes bankrupt, such as the demise of Eastman Kodak. However, as surprising as it may sound, even in cases like that, long-term owners can end up making money due to a combination of dividends, spin-offs, and tax credits.

PENNY STOCKS

Penny stocks are called many names, such as microcaps, small caps, stocks under $5, and more. But the one thing they share is that they're usually not listed on a major stock exchange and re□uire a totally different approach than other stocks.

Normal stocks are listed on NASDAQ, the New York Stock Exchange, and other major markets. Penny stocks, on the other hand, are often traded on the OTC, or Over the Counter, markets. This doesn't factor into the trade, however, and most online brokers support this market.

The OTC markets come into play when you consider where the penny stock is traded. The OTC Bulletin Board, an electronic trading service operated by the Financial Industry Regulatory Authority, requires all companies to meet the minimum standards of keeping up-to-date financial statements. Penny stocks listed on publications like the Pink Sheets may not have met these re□uirements, giving you less information to base your trading decisions on and carrying greater risk.

Penny stocks and low-priced shares are not right for everyone, despite the fact that they do have a lot of great attributes. They truly can turn a small investment into a large sum of money pretty quickly (but can just as □uickly wipe those dollars out).

For many people, the potential for big rewards does not outweigh the risks. Be honest with yourself, and do not feel bad about walking away from the entire concept. In general, this is often the best choice, because MOST situations involving penny stocks result in many investors taking losses.

The good news: the reason most are wasting their investment dollars is they are buying the wrong stocks, at the wrong prices, and usually for the wrong reasons. These investment risks can be easily avoided, mainly by learning a little bit about the reality of trading penny stocks, which this article will show you.

For example, the vast majority of investors buy penny stocks that trade on the over-the-counter (OTC) markets, and almost all of them will lose money. On the other hand, by getting involved with high-quality companies on the more serious and regulated exchanges, you pick investment choices from among legitimate and up-and-coming businesses.

These are mainly serious companies with proven business models. The penny stocks listed on the best markets just so happen to be very new, or still small, and so are trading for pennies... until they eventually trade for dollars.

How To Find The Best Ones

As we mentioned, trading penny stocks is risky. Many of these companies are fly-by-night and highly volatile, which puts traders in a position to lose big. However, you can still make money trading penny stocks if you trade smart and know what to look for.

What makes a penny stock a potential money-making stock? There are a few characteristics to look for:

- ✓ A company needs to make money. A company that loses money will always be a bad investment, no matter how low the share price is.

- ✓ A company needs substantial assets or cash. Strong businesses shouldn't need to liquidate future viability to appease creditors, because they have enough cash to account for contingencies.

✓ A company must have a strategy in place. Penny stock companies don't want to be penny stock companies, so the successful ones have a strategy in place to grow the business and get listed (or re-listed) on a major exchange. These goals should include rebuilding a long-term business and paying back investors.

HOW TO FIND GOOD PENNY STOCKS

Part of the challenge in determining how to make money trading penny stocks is finding them. Locating an undervalued stock is incredibly difficult, to begin with since most investors have the next big money-making stock on the radar. With penny stocks, you'll also need to find the undervalued stock that has a positive value, strong financials, and a promising outlook.

To make money selling the penny stocks, you first need to find someone to sell it at the bargain price. If a company turnaround is expected, a trader is going to hold on to shares to reap the rewards, which makes these shares more difficult for you to buy.

Once you've purchased the potentially lucrative penny stock, you also have to be sure you can turn around and sell it. You can always hold on to it and take a chance on it being hot in the future, but you got it for a bargain because it's not hot right now. No one is looking to buy it.

Considering all of this, the best hope of making money with penny stocks is finding the hidden gem, buying it at a bargain price, and holding on to it until the company rebuilds and gets back on a major market exchange again.

Using Scanners To Find Penny Stocks

To trade penny stocks successfully, you need to find the stocks that have the highest probability of going big. For many traders, scanners are the best way to do that.

Traders use stock screeners to narrow a huge list of available stocks to a small list with the characteristics they're looking for. By applying a filter to the stock screener list, you're left with only the stocks that fit your parameters. Popular filters include chart patterns, price, performance, and volatility, all of which can help you find the stocks with the greatest potential for a big run.

Three specific parameters to find these stocks are:

✓ **Breaking news**. Look for stocks that are gapping up because of a news break that could be lucrative for the company. Avoid stocks that have publicity from a buyout or something similar, however, because that usually means a breakeven or a loss for the shares.

- ✓ **Float**. The float is the number of shares actually available to trade, which is calculated by subtracting the closely held shares from insiders, employees, and the company's stock ownership plan. Ideally, you want the float to be below 100 million shares, but 50 million is even better. When a stock has fewer shares to trade, there's more buying interest that could drive the price up.
- ✓ **High relative volume**. The relative volume is an indicator that tells traders how the current volume compares to the past trading volumes over a specified period of time,

which gives you an idea of how "in-play" a particular stock is. The higher the relative volume, the more traders are watching and trading it, giving it plenty of liquidity for you to trade.

After you create your watchlist according to this criteria, you can wait for the market to open and see if there's a breakout over pre-market highs for an entry point, or wait for a bullish flag pattern, which signals a move higher.

Reading Stock Chart Patterns

Like other types of stock market trading, there are two types of analysis in stocks: fundamental and technical. Fundamental analysis uses information about the company itself, such as management, debts, contracts, lawsuits, and revenues, while technical analysis uses patterns on a trading chart.

Fundamental analysis is the preferred method of most traders, though a combination of both analyses can prove more beneficial than using one over the other. Once you find high-quality companies, technical analysis can give you plenty of insight into the underlying shares.

The relative strength index is a momentum oscillator that measures the speed and change of price movements on a scale of zero to 100. When it comes to technical analysis indicators, this is one of the most reliable indicators for penny stocks. Traditional interpretation and usage of the relative strength index use values of 70 or above to indicate the stock is overbought or overvalued, which may mean a trend reversal or pullback is coming. A value of 30 or below is interpreted as indicating a stock that's oversold or undervalued, which may signal a trend change or corrective price reversal on the up.

Here are some of the most reliable patterns to look for:

✓ **Bottoming-out patterns**. Bottoming-out patterns are another reliable way of assessing penny stocks. This pattern emerges after a long, sustained slide in the share price. The trend goes downward over several months, then goes sideways for a few weeks. When this occurs in conjunction with a sudden increase in trading volume, the shares are expected to enter a sustained recovery in price. This is especially true if it occurs with an oversold position.

✓ **Price dips**. Penny stocks are thinly traded so that they can have incredible price volatility due to the imbalance in buy and sell orders. This can lead to shares dipping significantly when the sellers outweigh the buyers. If a stock suddenly drops without any discernible reason and on a low trading volume, this is a price dip pattern. Price dips provide an opportunity, however, because they typically reverse. Taking advantage of price dips is all about being in the right place at the right time, keeping a buy order on a thinly-traded penny stock that's well below the recent price, and getting some of these shares at a lower price.

✓ **Top-out pattern**. A top-out pattern has similar principles as the bottoming-out pattern but in reverse. With this pattern, shares have been climbing for long periods of time, but appear to be levelling off or turning sideways. Sometimes this is just a short break before moving back up, but if it occurs with a penny stock, especially alongside a declining daily trading volume and overbought condition, others may be preparing to move in on it. Shareholders are looking to sell to capture the high prices while buying ends, leading to tumbling share prices.

- ✓ **Share consolidation**. The share consolidation is when a base of shareholders turns over, and it's a great sign for penny stock prices. Stockholders have high expectations for the share they bought, so they intend to hold on to them. The frustrated shareholders are looking to get out, however, so there's a transformation happening. The penny stock will trade sideways on a higher-than-average volume, which is a bullish indicator for the future of the shares. The stocks will reach a tipping point when there are no more sellers looking to get out and a small percentage of owners holding on, so the next move for the stock is high.

✓ **Candlestick chart patterns**. Candlestick chart patterns are uni□ue in that they can show if a penny stock's trend is about to reverse, or if prices may rise or fall in the short term. Candlestick chart patterns speak to investor psychology, which has an incredible impact on the state of the market.

Generally, candlestick patterns are a great way to confirm the existence of other patterns.

✓ **Gapping.** Gapping is when a share opens higher or lower than it traded the day before. If a shared gap higher, it's a bullish indicator, and if it gaps lower, it's a bearish indicator. This is a technical indicator that can be misleading, but it still has enough validity to belong in your arsenal of penny stock strategy.

✓ **Going against the trend**. Going against the trend is one of the most reliable technical indicators with any type of stock shares, but it works incredibly well for penny stocks in particular, due to its ability to identify stocks that perform well under pressure. If the market as a whole has significant dips and a specific industry sees a drop, the shares that stay steady in price are the ones standing to gain when the market recovers. For example, if the shares you're watching fall only slightly, stay steady, or even increase in price while the rest of the stocks are going downhill, that's a bullish sign for that stock.

Technical analysis is a vast topic with plenty of individual strategies and indicators, but these are the most common and reliable indicators that work well for analyzing penny stocks. Just be sure to remember that they aren't infallible and should be worked into a larger strategy.

Using Financial Ratios

Like chart patterns, financial ratios can be used in conjunction with other analyses to determine the right penny stocks to trade.

With ade☐uate financial disclosure, which shouldn't be a problem with more reputable penny stock companies, the same analytical methods used for larger companies can be used to assess the worth of a penny stock. A positive trend on the balance sheet and strong numbers are important because so much of a penny stock's value is based on projected performance.

- ✓ **Li☐uidity ratios**. Li☐uidity ratios, which include the ☐uick ratio, cash ratio, and current ratio, are the first ratios that you should consider in analyzing penny stocks. Penny stocks can't always cover their short-term liabilities within a given time frame. Lower li☐uidity ratios are a good indication that a company is struggling to stay in business or grow.

- ✓ **Leverage ratios**. Leverage ratios are another important subset of ratios. These are similar to li□uidity ratios in that they focus on a company's ability to cover its debt, though this pertains to long-term debt and is broken down into debt ratios and interest coverage ratios. Debt ratios will shrink or expand, but expanding ratios should only occur if the company is trying to support future growth and development. Interest coverage ratios measure the debt load and the company's ability to manage it, so higher interest coverage ratios are preferable.

- ✓ **Performance ratios**. Performance ratios include subsets like gross profit margin, net profit margin, and return on assets. This helps □uantifies money made at each level of the income statement, which should reflect steady and sustainable growth in operating earnings.

✓ **Valuation ratios**. Valuation ratios measure the appeal of the stock at the current price. In the case of penny stocks, stock shares can be undervalued. Price-to-earnings ratio is the most common ratio for stocks, but it becomes meaningless if a company's earnings are zero or negative. With penny stocks that fall into this category, the price-to-sales and price-to-cash-flow ratios are more effective.

These financial ratios can be calculated and compared to the same ratios for previous periods or projected ratios, as well as ratios of direct competitors or the overall market to gauge the company's value.

Minimize Risk With Your Trading

Do penny stocks really make money? Yes, but they can also lose a lot of money. Penny stocks are a risky investment, but there are some ways to lower the risk and put yourself in a position for money-making penny stock trading.

- ✓ Pick stocks from companies in the OTCQX tier of the OTC markets, because this tier has stricter financial standards for listed companies. These companies must comply with the U.S. securities laws and meet higher standards of operations compared to OTCQB and OTC Pink markets.
- ✓ Avoid Pink Sheet stocks, which are prone to manipulation and fraud. The most reputable companies are not only more likely to give you a return,

73

but they're also a less risky investment.

✓ Avoid pump-and-dump scammers. Many OTC penny stocks will be promoted as the next big breakout, but the reality is that these large companies that provide a near-guarantee of success start with a high-priced IPO, not on the penny stock market.

✓ Avoid li□uidity penny stocks. Most penny stocks have a volume of around thousands of shares a day, but penny stock companies with breaking news could have a high volume of millions of shares in a day. How do penny stocks make money for you? This is the time when you're likely to cash in, and in the penny stock world, there's some major event nearly every day.

- ✓ Don't overtrade. Once you find the stocks you want, buy where you think other traders will enter, know when to sell penny stocks, take quick profits, and adjust the stops for small gains that add up over time. You may get lucky and have a big win on occasion, but most of your money will come from these smaller trades.
- ✓ Focus on trading and not investing. Trade penny stocks every day, and you'll find that you're making money from buying and selling penny stocks, rather than investing in the next big hit. Added up over weeks, months, and years, you'll find that you're raking in cash.

JUNK BONDS

Junk bonds are corporate bonds that are high-risk and high-return. They have been rated as not investment grade by Standard & Poor's or Moody's because the company that issues them is not fiscally sound. These bonds tend to have the highest return, compared to other bonds, to compensate for the additional risk. That is why they are also called high-yield bonds. The junk bond market gives you an early indication of how much risk investors are willing to take on. If investors get out of junk bonds, that means they are becoming more risk-averse and don't feel optimistic about the economy. That predicts a market correction, a bear market, or a contraction in the business cycle.

On the other hand, if junk bonds are being bought, it means investors are becoming more confident about the economy and are willing to take on more risk. That forecasts a market upturn, a bull market, or economic expansion.

In a nutshell, junk bonds operate much like any other band instrument in the market. By investing in one, you are lending money to the issuer. In return, you will receive a fixed rate of interest until the bonds mature. At the end of the term, you will then receive your original investment back. However, junk bonds are perceived as high-risk by the financial markets.

By this, we mean that there is a much greater chance that the issuer will either default on their interest payments or, worse, default on the principal. Although there are different rating systems that determine whether a bond should be classed as 'junk,' this is usually based on the ratings issued by Standard & Poors. If the bond issuer in Question carries a credit rating of less than BB, then Standard & Poor's will classify the investment as a junk bond.

In order to set the scene, let's look at a Quick example of how a junk bond investment might work.

Example of a Junk Bond Investment

- ✓ You invest $10,000 in a corporate bond with a Standard & Poor's rating of 'C.'
- ✓ This means that the bond is classified as a junk bond
- ✓ The junk bond has a yield of 8% and a term of 5 years
- ✓ At the end of each year, your 8% interest pays $800

- ✓ Over the course of 5 years, your total interest amounts to $4,000 (5 x $800)
- ✓ At the end of the term, you then get your original $10,000 back

As you can see from the above example, you made a juicy $4,000 from your junk bond investment over the 5-year term. Although the annual yield amounted to 8%, you actually got an ROI (Return-on-Investment) of 40%, which is very attractive. However, the reason that you were able to get such an attractive yield is that the bonds fall within the junk category.

As such, although in this example, you received your interest and principal back in full, this might not always be the case. On the contrary, the issuer behind the junk bond could default if they run in to further financial difficulties.

Ratings

Junk bonds are rated by Moody's and Standard & Poors as being speculative. That means the company's ability to avoid default is outweighed by uncertainties. That includes the company's exposure to bad business or economic conditions.

A rating of Ba or BB is less speculative than a C rating. Most junk bonds are rated B. Here are the different ratings:

- ✓ High Risk - Rated Ba or B by Moody's and BB or B by Standard & Poors. The company currently is able to meet payments, but probably won't if economic or business conditions worsen. That's because it's unusually vulnerable to adverse conditions.

- ✓ Highest Risk - Rated Caa, Ca, or C by Moody's, and CCC, CC, or C by Standard & Poors. Business and economic conditions must be favourable for the company to avoid default.

- ✓ In Default - Rated C by Moody's and D by Standard & Poors. These are currently in default.

Investors categorize junk bonds as either "Fallen Angels" or "Rising Stars." The former are bonds that were initially investment grade. Credit agencies lowered the rating when the company's credit worsened. "Rising Stars" are junk bonds whose ratings were raised because the company's credit improved. They may eventually become investment-grade bonds.

The federal government guarantees Treasurys. Junk bonds make up the debt of 95 per cent of U.S. companies with revenues over $35 million. These make up 100 per cent of the debt of companies with revenues lower than that—for example, familiar companies like U.S. Steel, Delta, and Dole Foods issue junk bonds.

Why Would A Person Invest In Junk Bonds?

Junk bonds are a good investment for those who need a higher return and can afford the higher risk. Even then, it's advisable to only buy them in the expansion phase of the business cycle. You could then take advantage of the higher return with the minimum amount of risk.

How To Buy Junk Bonds

You can purchase junk bonds either individually or through a high yield fund through your financial adviser. Funds are the best way to go for individual investors because they are run by managers with the specialized knowledge needed to pick the right bonds. Keep in mind that many funds forbid you from withdrawing your investment for the first year or two.

Another way to invest is through junk bond exchange-traded funds. The two biggest are HYG and JNK.

ADVANTAGES OF JUNK BONDS

Junk bonds can boost overall returns in your portfolio while avoiding the higher volatility of stocks. First, they offer higher yields than investment-grade bonds. Second, they have the opportunity to do even better if they are upgraded when the business does improve. Because of this, junk bonds are not highly correlated to other bonds.

Junk bonds are highly correlated to stocks but also provide fixed interest payments. Bondholders get paid before stockholders in case of bankruptcy.

Another advantage is that they are issued with 10-year terms, or less, and can be called after four to five years. Junk bonds perform best in the expansion phase of the business cycle. That's because the underlying companies are less likely to default when times are good. A good economy reduces risk.

DISADVANTAGES OF JUNK BONDS

If the business defaults, you'll lose 100 per cent of your initial investment. That means you need to analyze the credit risk of each company. If you invest in high-yield mutual funds instead, the manager does that before purchasing any bonds.

Another disadvantage is that even credit-worthy companies can get caught by negative economic trends. They have the cash flow to pay their debts at existing interest rates. But some of their colleagues default on their bonds. This sends the interest rates skyrocketing on all bonds in their industry. When it comes time to refinance, they can no longer afford the higher rates.

Junk bonds are vulnerable to interest rate increases. If the yield curve flattens, banks are less willing to lend. That's because they borrow on the short-term money markets and lend on the long-term bond and mortgage market. Speculative companies won't be able to refinance or issue new bonds. The prospect of the Fed raising rates in December threw investors into a panic mode.

VOLATILITY

Volatility is a statistical measure of the dispersion of returns for a given security or market index. In most cases, the higher the volatility, the riskier the security. Volatility is often measured as either the standard deviation or variance between returns from that same security or market index.

In the securities markets, volatility is often associated with big swings in either direction. For example, when the stock market rises and falls more than one per cent over a sustained period of time, it is called a "volatile" market. An asset's volatility is a key factor when pricing options contracts.

Volatility often refers to the amount of uncertainty or risk related to the size of changes in a security's value. A higher volatility means that a security's value can potentially be spread out over a larger range of values. This means that the price of the security can change dramatically over a short time period in either direction. A lower volatility means that a security's value does not fluctuate dramatically, and tends to be more steady.

One way to measure an asset's variation is to quantify the daily returns (per cent move on a daily basis) of the asset. Historical volatility is based on historical prices and represents the degree of variability in the returns of an asset. This number is without a unit and is expressed as a percentage. While variance captures the dispersion of returns around the mean of an asset in general, volatility is a measure of that variance bounded by a specific period of time. Thus, we can report daily volatility, weekly, monthly, or annualized volatility. It is, therefore, useful to think of volatility as the annualized standard deviation: Volatility = $\sqrt{}$ (variance annualized)

HOW TO TRADE STOCK MARKET VOLATILITY

Trading stock market volatility successfully involves effective hedging, knowing when to sell stocks, employing sound risk management, and spotting buying opportunities when renowned stocks see a fall in price.

Hedging

Hedging against spikes in volatility is important to offset losses. This can be done by buying put options, which allow the sale of assets at an agreed price on or before a particular date, and trading inverse exchange-traded funds, which act as the inverse of the index or benchmark it tracks. Traders can also explore aggregated stocks through an index to protect against volatility.

Selling stock/managing risk

If extreme volatility is affecting your mindset, it may be wise to sell off some stock and put your money into less dynamic securities. This leaves you free to trade another day without risking more than you are prepared to lose.

Practising sound risk management is essential when dealing with aggressive price action. Volatile stocks can lose you a lot of money and should not be traded if your mindset isn't right that day, particularly if day trading.

Spotting buying opportunities

Sometimes a buying opportunity arises when high volatility hits the price of high-quality stocks. For example, in early 2019, the NASDAQ and S&P 500 constituent Apple cut its earnings forecast, leading to its price dropping 10-15% in the following days. However, just three months later, it completely recovered and approached a $1 trillion valuation once more. Identifying opportunities to go long when the market conditions reverse is one-way traders look to speculate when coupled with prudent trade management techni ues.

Volatile stocks for day trading

Like the most volatile currency pairs, volatile stocks can show significant movement throughout the day, making them potentially an attractive option for day traders. While some stocks may move 0.5% in a single day, others may move as far as 5% in the same period, meaning traders should be constantly alert.

To find a volatile stock for day trading, watch a stock you found with your stock screener for intraday movement. If a stock opens down 10% and starts moving, as opposed to staying static, it is being day traded and may be worth consideration.

Due to the speed of price movement, executing day trades can be a physical endeavour, and good reflexes win the day.

Volatile Stocks for Swing Trading

Swing traders hold positions for more than a day, making the effects of volatility potentially smaller than when day trading. Stocks that may be suitable for swing trading include large-cap stocks such as Apple, Facebook, and Microsoft, because they have a large volume of shares changing hands at any given point.

FOREX TRADING

Forex, also known as foreign exchange, FX, or currency trading, is a decentralized global market where all the world's currencies trade. The forex market is the largest, most li□uid market in the world, with an average daily trading volume exceeding $5 trillion. All the world's combined stock markets don't even come close to this. But what does that mean to you? Take a closer look at forex trading, and you may find some exciting trading opportunities unavailable with other investments.

What Is The Forex Market?

The foreign exchange market is where currencies are traded. Currencies are important to most people around the world, whether they realize it or not because currencies need to be exchanged in order to conduct foreign trade and business. If you are living in the U.S. and want to buy cheese from France, either you or the company that you buy the cheese from has to pay the French for the cheese in euros (EUR). This means that the U.S. importer would have to exchange the equivalent value of U.S. dollars (USD) into euros. The same goes for travelling. A French tourist in Egypt can't pay in euros to see the pyramids because it's not the locally accepted currency. As such, the tourist has to exchange the euros for the local currency, in this case, the Egyptian pound, at the current exchange rate.

One unique aspect of this international market is that there is no central marketplace for foreign exchange. Rather, currency trading is conducted electronically over-the-counter (OTC), which means that all transactions occur via computer networks between traders around the world, rather than on one centralized exchange. The market is open 24 hours a day, five and a half days a week, and currencies are traded worldwide in the major financial centres of London, New York, Tokyo, Zurich, Frankfurt, Hong Kong, Singapore, Paris, and Sydney—across almost every time zone. This means that when the trading day in the U.S. ends, the forex market begins anew in Tokyo and Hong Kong. As such, the forex market can be extremely active at any time of the day, with price ⬜uotes changing constantly.

Currency as an Asset Class
There are two distinct features to currencies as an asset class:
- ✓ You can earn the interest rate differential between two currencies.

✓ You can profit from changes in the exchange rate.

An investor can profit from the difference between two interest rates in two different economies by buying the currency with the higher interest rate and shorting the currency with the lower interest rate. Prior to the 2008 financial crisis, it was very common to short the Japanese yen (JPY) and buy British pounds (GBP) because the interest rate differential was very large. This strategy is sometimes referred to as a "carry trade."

Why We Can Trade Currencies

Currency trading was very difficult for individual investors prior to the internet. Most currency traders were large multinational corporations, hedge funds, or high-net-worth individuals because forex trading re□uired a lot of capital. With help from the internet, a retail market aimed at individual traders has emerged, providing easy access to the foreign exchange markets, either through the banks themselves or brokers making a secondary market. Most online brokers or dealers offer very high leverage to individual traders who can control a large trade with a small account balance.

BENEFITS OF FOREX TRADING

With the huge growth of trading opportunities over the past two decades, financial markets have become accessible to more and more people, who are faced with the challenge of choosing the market most suitable to them. Any potential trader must take into consideration the advantages and drawbacks of a financial market before they commit their time and resources to it. In the case of currency trading, the resources re□uired for a beginner to get started are relatively low, and it is much more flexible in terms of time commitment, so forex is often the market of choice for novices and pros alike. If you already know what is a forex and how forex works, you can explore the top 10 benefits of forex trading below, among many other advantages that you'll discover on your trading journey.

Largest Financial Market

The foreign exchange (forex) market is the largest financial market in the world, and it's not going to cede that title anytime soon. It's not hard to see why the forex market is used as a snapshot of global trade and economic activity. On average, between $4 and 5 trillion (yes, that's trillion with a T) is traded daily. That's about $200 billion an hour, $3 billion a minute, $50 million a second. And with traders of all sorts participating from all over the world, it truly is the single most accessible and global trading market.

It's for Everyone

Forex trading isn't just for the big shots. Getting started as a forex trader doesn't cost a lot of money, especially when compared to trading stocks or options, and it's part of its appeal to a large number of people globally. Even without much start-up capital, forex trading is accessible to the average individual. E□uity offers trading accounts with only $500 minimum deposit, and leverage up to 1:500 is available*. This doesn't mean that you'll be a good trader right away, it does take time and trial to learn and become skilful, so it's advisable to take it slow and warm your way in. Read our forex education section to build your trading knowledge.

High Volume and Liquidity

The forex market is enormous; we've got that. But why is this such a good thing? One word – liquidity. What this means is that given the large volume being traded at any given moment, under normal market conditions, you don't have to wait. With a click, you can buy and sell as you please, since there will usually be someone on the other end willing to trade back. You can even automate your trading. Of course, the market does have its quiet hours, but generally, there are always trades to be made, especially if trading popular pairs like USD/EUR and other majors.

Nobody Owns the Market

Given the sheer size of the forex market and the number of participants, no single institutional trader (no matter how big) can control market prices for an extended time period. The market □uickly calibrates itself and levels the playing field. Additionally, the forex market is decentralized, and there are no middlemen. You trade directly with another participant in the market, and a retail forex broker simply facilitates this connection. Essentially the market is influenced directly by the economy itself, not one person or a company. You can't corner it, and you can't control it, and that means that you're not as small a fish as you may think.

Trade the Highs and the Lows

No matter if the market is rising or falling, you can trade, and some forex trading strategies even depend on the latter. You can find opportunities in any market condition, and you can trade when you believe the price of a currency pair is going up or when you anticipate it going down. Some traders even thrive on high volatility periods. Although carrying more risk, these sudden price changes can be advantageous if timed right. Whether you're following longer market trends or trading day to day movements, there is plenty of trading opportunity to be found.

A 24-Hour Market

The forex market never sleeps. Open 24 hours a day, five days a week, you can trade whenever you want to, not when the market dictates. There is no waiting for the opening bell or scrambling to get your order executed before a daily close. Trading begins with the opening of the Sydney session and closes with the New York session, by which time it starts all over again, round the clock. This means you can be as active or passive as you'd like, and trade on your own schedule – be it morning, noon,   or   night.

Low Transaction Costs

As mentioned above, the difference between the bid and ask price is the broker's spread, and this is the retail transaction cost. Highly capitalized brokers can offer very competitive spreads, thus minimizing your trading costs and maximizing your profits. Equity offers an average spread of 1.5 pips** for its Executive account type and 0.4 pips** for a Premiere account. It's important to understand how spreads are measured. For example, if GBP/USD has a bid price of 1.55310 and an asking price of 1.55313, the spread is 0.3 pips.

Leverage

A small deposit can go a long way. With leverage, you can essentially "borrow money" from your broker to trade with in excess of your actual deposited funds. This is a powerful tool and one of the most attractive features of forex trading. E□uity offers up to 1:500 leverage, which gives you increased buying power and can mean larger gains, but it also carries the risk of larger losses. Please be sure to fully understand the risks of trading with leverage before you use it.

Risk-free Demo Account

You can make use of a free forex demo account to practice forex trading and learn the ropes. Trading with a demo account is just like the real thing, but you're doing it with "play money." A demo account is great for those who want to test the waters or improve their trading skills in real market conditions without risking any actual capital. And this is all for free and without any commitment. So give it a try and see the benefits of trading forex for yourself!

FOREX TRADING EXAMPLES

To help you understand how forex trading works, view our CFD examples below, which take you through both buying and selling scenarios.

CFD Trading Example 1: Buying EUR/GBP
EUR/GBP is trading at 0.84950 / 0.84960.

You decide to buy €20,000 because you think the price of EUR/GBP will go up. EUR/GBP has a margin rate of 3.34%, which means that you only have to deposit 3.34% of the total position value as a position margin. Therefore, in this example your position margin will be £567.50 (3.34% x [€20,000 x 0.84955]).

Remember that if the price moves against you, it is possible to lose more than your initial position margin of £567.50.

Outcome A: winning trade
Your prediction was correct, and the price rises over the next hour to 0.85530 / 0.85540. You decide to close your long trade by selling at 0.85530 (the current sell price).

The price has moved 57 points (0.85530 − 0.84960) in your favour.
Your profit is ([€20,000 x 0.85530] − [€20,000 x 0.84960]) = £114.

Outcome B: losing trade
Unfortunately, your prediction was wrong, and the price of EUR/GBP drops over the next hour to 0.84390 / 0.84400. You feel the

price is likely to continue dropping, so to limit the losses, you decide to sell at 0.84390 (the current sell price) to close the trade.

The price has moved 57 points (0.84960 – 0.84390) against you.

Your loss is ([€20,000 x 0.84960] – [€20,000 x 0.84390]) = –£114.

CFD Trading Example 2: Selling EUR/USD

EUR/USD is trading at 1.13010 / 1.13020.

Let's assume poor German manufacturing data indicates that the euro is likely to fall against the US dollar in the coming days. You decide to sell €20,000 because you think the price of EUR/USD will go down.

EUR/USD has a margin rate of 3.34%, which means that you only have to deposit

3.34% of the total position value as a position margin. Therefore, in this example your position margin will be $754.94 (3.34% x [€20,000 x 1.13015]). The platform will automatically convert the position margin amount into your account currency at the prevailing CMC Markets conversion rate.

Remember that if the price moves against you, it is possible to lose more than your initial position margin of $754.94.

Outcome A: winning trade

Your prediction was correct, and EUR/USD drops over the next hour to 1.12510 / 1.12520. You decide to close your short trade by buying at 1.12520 (the current buy price).

The price has moved 49 points (1.13010 − 1.12520) in your favour.

Your profit is ([€20,000 x 1.13010] – [€20,000 x 1.12520]) = $98.

Outcome B: losing trade
Unfortunately, your prediction was wrong, and the price of EUR/USD rises over the next hour to

1.13800 / 1.13810. You feel the price is likely to continue rising, so to limit your losses, you decide to buy at 1.13810 (the current buy price) to close the trade.

The price has moved 80 points (1.13810 – 1.13010) against you.
Your loss is ([€20,000 x 1.13810] – [€20,000 x 1.13010]) = –$160.

OPTION TRADING

Options trading is simply trading options and is typically done with securities on the stock or bond market (as well as ETFs and the like).

For starters, you can only buy or sell options through a brokerage like E*Trade (ETFC) - Get Report or Fidelity (FNF) - Get Report.

When buying a call option, the strike price of an option for a stock, for example, will be determined based on the current price of that stock. For example, if a share of a given stock (like Amazon (AMZN) - Get Report) is $1,748, any strike price (the price of the call option) that is above that share price is considered to be "out of the money." Conversely, if the strike price is under the current share price of the stock, it's considered "in the money."

However, for put options (right to sell), the opposite is true - with strike prices below the current share price being considered "out of the money" and vice versa. And, what's more important - any "out of the money" options (whether call or put options) are worthless at expiration (so you really want to have an "in the money" option when trading on the stock market).

Another way to think of it is that call options are generally bullish, while put options are generally bearish.

Options typically expire on Fridays with different time frames (for example, monthly, bi-monthly, ⬜uarterly, etc.). Many options contracts are for six months.

Pros And Cons

Some of the major pros of options trading revolve around their supposed safety.

Options are often more resilient to changes (and downturns) in market prices, can help increase income on current and future investments, can often get you better deals on a variety of eᐨuities and, perhaps most importantly, can help you capitalize on that eᐨuity rising or dropping over time without having to invest in it directly.

Of course, there are cons to trading options - including risk.

There are a variety of ways to interpret risks associated with options trading, but these risks primarily revolve around the levels of volatility or uncertainty of the market. For example, expensive options are those whose uncertainty is high - meaning the market is volatile for that particular asset, and it is riskier to trade it.

Options Trading Strategies

When trading options, the contracts will typically take this form:

Stock ticker (name of the stock), date of expiration (typically in mm/dd/yyyy, although sometimes dates are flipped with the year first, month second and day last), the strike price, call or put, and the premium price (for example, $3). So an example of a call option for Apple stock would look something like this: APPL 01/15/2018 200 Call @ 3.

Still, depending on what platform you are trading on, the option trade will look very different.

There are numerous strategies you can employ when options trading - all of which vary on risk, reward, and other factors. And while there are dozens of strategies (most of them fairly complicated), here are a few main strategies that have been recommended for beginners.

Options Trading Examples

There are lots of examples of options trading that largely depend on which strategy you are using. However, as a basic idea of what a typical call or put option would be, let's consider a trader buying a call and put option on Microsoft (MSFT).

For example, if you bought a long call option (remember, a call option is a contract that gives you the right to buy shares later on) for 100 shares of Microsoft stock at $110 per share for December 1, you would have the right to buy 100 shares of that stock at $110 per share regardless of if the stock price changed or not by December 1. For this long call option, you would be expecting the price of Microsoft to increase, thereby letting you reap the profits when you are able to buy it at a cheaper cost than its market value. However, if you decide not

113

to exercise that right to buy the shares, you would only be losing the premium you paid for the option since you aren't obligated to buy any shares.

If you were buying a long put option for Microsoft, you would be betting that the price of Microsoft shares would decrease up until your contract expires, so that, if you chose to exercise your right to sell those shares, you'd be selling them at a higher price than their market value.

Another example involves buying a long call option for a $2 premium (so for the 100 shares per contract, that would equal $200 for the whole contract). You buy an option for 100 shares of Oracle (ORCL) for a strike price of $40 per share, which expires in two months, expecting the stock to go to $50 by that time. You've spent $200 on the contract (the $2 premium times 100 shares for the contract). When the stock price hits $50 as you bet it would, your call option to buy at $40 per share will be $10 "in the money" (the contract is now worth $1,000 since you have 100 shares of the stock) - since the difference between 40 and 50 is 10. At this point, you can exercise your call option and buy the stock at $40 per share instead of the $50 it is now worth - making your $200 original contract now worth $1,000 - which is an $800 profit and a 400% return.

CONCLUSION

You can make a lot of money investing in stocks or trading in the stock market, but it is not something for the new investors. Care must be taken when it comes to stock investments. The investor must have a solid understanding of stocks and how they trade in the market or risk losing money in a volatile type of investment.

Every investment is inherently connected with risk. Its existence and diversity among various types of investments are one of the driving forces behind the development of the capital market. The risk has also caused the emergence and development of alternative investments. Flourishment of this segment of the market has also been influenced by periodical financial crises, which have been the driving force behind the search for investments that would allow investment portfolio diversification and would provide opportunities for profiting, even during price declines on the market.

Alternative investments constitute an effective tool for risk diversification; however, they are not suitable for all investors. Institutional investors, including the banks, pension funds, large companies, as well as individual investors within the wealth management sector, constitute a dominant group of the investors on the alternative investments market. Investors considering such investments should rely on their own preferences regarding the acceptable risk as well as on the entities acting as the trustees of the investors' assets. Often, it is the experience gained during the management of its own alternative investment portfolio, which allows verification and assessment of the acceptable level of the risk, the definition of the maximum loss tolerance, and the designation of achievable financial targets.

This book aims to present alternative investments in the management of the investors' assets. Analysis of this sector of the global financial market is not possible without determining which alternative investment categories can be □ualified within this group. There is still no universal definition of alternative investments that would be agreed on in the financial world and which would indicate a set of homogenous characteristics that are relatively stable over time. As a result, many individual and institutional investors are not fully convinced that 'alternative investments' constitute a separate category of investments. The multitude of various definitions raises the need for the creation of some universal patterns, which would allow correct classification of individual investments and at, the same time, would make it easier to manage them.

Do not go yet; one last thing to do

If you enjoyed this book or found it useful, I'd be very grateful if you'd post a short review on Amazon. Your support really does make a difference, and I read all the reviews personally so I can get your feedback and make this book even better.

Thanks again for your support!

fff

www.ingramcontent.com/pod-product-compliance
Lightning Source LLC
Chambersburg PA
CBHW030946240526
45463CB00016B/1978